Flinch!

Being Brave in Today's Culture

Don't Flinch!

Ron Brown

ISBN 1-929478-38-0

Cross Training Publishing
317 West Second Street
Grand Island, NE 68801
(308) 384-5762

This book is manufactured in the United States of America.Library of Congress Cataloging in Publication Data in Progress.

The views expressed in this book, are Ron Brown's opinions and not necessarily those of either the University of Nebraska or any other institution. All royalties of this book go to Mission Nebraska

Don't Flinch! Webster defines the word "flinch" as to withdraw or shrink from, as if from pain. Throughout this message you will be challenged by Ron Brown to not withdraw or shrink from your responsibilities in today's culture—to stand by your values despite the pain or cost to you personally. Ron gave this message during the spring of 2001, in Grand Island to a crowd of more than 1,000 students and adults. This book is based on Ron's speech that evening which led to several hundred people responding to his message. We encourage you to read this book as if you were part of that evening.

Let's think about a familiar scene for nearly 80,000 football fans that will be dressed in red this fall. The opening home game in Memorial Stadium will probably be hot! Not just on the field but the stands will be buzzing with excitement as fans anticipate the opening kick off. As the music starts, you notice that Frank Solich and the Husker players are about to take the field. People are standing and cheering. You're getting goose bumps from the excitement. Suddenly, the Huskers burst onto the field, but something is missing. You notice that the players aren't wearing their normal equipment. There are no helmets, no shoulder pads. They have on little shorts and a little band around their waist with two flags attached to it. When you bought that football ticket, did you expect to see a bunch of guys playing flag football?

Have you ever played flag football? It's fun, isn't it? But, would it be fun to watch Eric Crouch, a great quarterback, play flag football? You know what I think? The fans would be disappointed because that's not what they came to watch. They paid to watch tackle football. They want the players to wear helmets and pads so they can crash into each other. Watching a bunch of guys in shorts pulling each other's flags isn't much of a spectator sport.

Sometimes our faith in God is like playing flag football. You know, someone pulls the little flag and we stop. We don't want to make a big issue of our faith. Our faith is fun and games, reserved for Sunday morning at church or maybe a Wednesday night if we are a bit more serious. Our faith is a small portion of our life that we don't display in the public square. Hogwash! You know what? God expects everyone to put on shoulder pads and helmets, line up, and run full speed because our faith in Christ is important!

We are in a spiritual battle. We have an opponent that hates us! God can handle it by Himself. God could take the field and destroy the opponent; instead, He says, "I'm the coach and you are the players and I'm going to delegate game responsibilities to you. I will empower you, but you've got to be willing to put on the shoulder pads and helmet and go out there and collide with your opponent."

God loves impact players. We do, too, don't we? Mike Brown plays for the Chicago Bears. I had the opportunity to recruit Mike Brown in high school to the University of Nebraska, so I've known him since he was a junior in high school. Mike was only 5-feet-8 and barely 180 pounds when he graduated from high school, but when I watched his recruiting tape, he moved around the football field like a rocket! There was never any hesitation when he tackled another player. Not once did I see him flinch when driving his body into a ball carrier.

Not many players tackle like Mike Brown. That's why he is such a great player. Some players, just before they make contact, flinch and turn their head and shoulders a little bit. They don't want to take the full blow. The natural tendency is to avoid pain and wince. It's perhaps the most difficult thing to teach young football players. However, if they don't keep from flinching, they will always hurt both the team and themselves. Many of the head and neck injuries in football are from players that have ducked their heads when trying to avoid a collision. Football coaches know that they must teach their players to keep their heads up when making contact. Coaches are constantly reminding their players that it's better to take the blow at full speed with proper technique than to avoid the contact by flinching.

We don't expect anything less from our Husker football players, do we? Every fan wants his favorite player to crash into the opposition full speed. Football players are responsible for colliding into their opponents full speed. That is exactly what God is wanting from us spiritually. He wants full speed players. He wants players that won't flinch or wince from their responsibilities.

Tonight, I will be sharing a message about being brave in today's culture. A message about being an impact player for Christ. Prepare to be challenged!

God's Impact Player

Now, there is a guy I want to talk to you about who was a big time player for the Lord. His name was Paul. He was an impact player for God. Paul wrote a portion of Scripture that reveals his heart. You will find that it definitely relates to your life. The Apostle Paul tells us in Romans 1:14-16 who he is. An impact player must know who he is. Now, I will contend with you that there are a lot of people walking around in life who don't know who they are. For example, some people say, "Oh, you are Coach Brown. You coach for the Huskers." They think that is who I am. That is not who I am. It's my job. Some people have been very nice to me because I'm a coach. I don't get all excited about it because I know they really don't know me. They like what I represent, as if a national championship is what it's all about. I have been on three national championship teams. We received rings, watches, sweatshirts, and trophies. I have stored them in a drawer. The only ring I've got on is my wedding ring. All these material things haven't solved one problem I've ever had. In fact, these national championships can leave you high and dry. Empty promises lurk behind these championships. Some of our players at Nebraska have been waiting on the NFL Draft the last few years. It seems everybody thinks they are going to be a first round draft pick. Do you know how many Huskers got drafted in the first round this year? Zero. Empty promises. Oh, we have had a few who went in the early rounds, but we have had a number of guys who were told they were going to be drafted who weren't drafted at all.

This world is full of empty promises. The culture raises standards of success for you and says, "You know what? You better jump up and hit our standards. If you don't, you are a failure." Consequently, there are a lot of people walking around who really don't know who they are. They are like puppets. The world is really pulling the strings for you. You spend your whole life chasing these empty pursuits, these empty promises. Then you come up empty and want to know why.

The Apostle Paul recognized the empty pursuits of the world. He also recognized that God had a plan and a purpose for him, and that God's promises are not empty. In the Bible, in Romans 1:14-16, Paul wrote three "I am" statements. He said," *I am* under obligation both to Greeks and to Barbarians, both to the wise and to the foolish, so for my part *I am* eager to preach the gospel to you who are in Rome, for *I am* not ashamed of the gospel. It is the power of God for salvation." Paul knew who he was.

Player Responsibilities

Why is Paul under obligation to people?

How can that be? Does anyone like being dictated to by people? Well, Paul was talking about a sense of obligation to people. He had a love for people. Paul was on a rescue mission because he recognized something important. The day he was knocked off his high horse, he recognized that Jesus is God, and the Messiah. He recognized that without knowing Jesus, he would be lost forever in a place called Hell, a place for losers, a place of empty promises and empty dreams for eternity.

So Paul said, "You know what? Not only have I been saved, but also I recognize that God wants everyone to be saved." Paul realized the reason he had breath in his body was to be on a rescue mission for people. He was obligated to people.

Are you obliged to people? Think about this: What happens if I walk out of this building tonight, and suddenly a car comes at me. The driver doesn't see me and I don't see him. Let's say this guy named Billy jumps out and knocks me out of the way of the oncoming car. The momentum of him thrusting me out of the way puts him right in the path of that car. The car hits him and kills him instantly. I turn around and realize that this person has just saved my life. Do you think I would be obliged to Billy? He may be dead and gone, but I would be obligated to his family and would want to know why he risked his life for me.

Let's say I walk into a coffee shop a couple days later, and somebody is talking about Billy. They are talking negatively about him, "That crazy guy sacrificed his life for some stranger. What a fool. He deserved to die." No doubt, I would jump up in their faces and say, "Hey, wait a minute. Let me tell you what he did. Let me tell you why I'm here today. I am the guy that he saved. I am obliged to this guy and I don't like you talking about him that way."

You know what? I would be obligated to all people at that point. I would recognize that anyone can die at any moment, and that is exactly the attitude that Paul had. Do you realize that you are here on a mission, a rescue mission, if you know Christ as your Savior and Lord? The reason you have breath in your body is because you are on a "rescue the lost" mission.

Look who Paul was rescuing. He said he

was obligated to Greeks and Jews. They hated one another. Though Paul was Jewish, he knew he was called to help the Greek people—and all others who are without Christ.

Look around when you leave this building tonight. There are people walking around who are going to Hell. Jesus made a statement that is incredible. He said in Matthew 7:13-14 that most people will go to Hell. They will reject Jesus Christ. Think about it. When was the last time you went to a funeral and the pastor said, "We are so sorry. Today, our dearly beloved has died and gone to Hell." I've never been to a funeral where someone hasn't "gone to Heaven," and I've been to a number of funerals. The truth is Jesus said statistically that most people are going to Hell.

Statistically, in this audience tonight, most of the people are going to Hell. They are going to reject the notion of Christ, reject the message of Christ, and most importantly, reject the person of Christ. They want to define God on their own terms.

Maybe some of you here are like Paul, who recognized he needed to get out and share with the lost. He was obligated to Barbarians. Who were Barbarians? Well, Paul had an experience with Barbarians in Acts 28. He and Luke were captives on a ship. They shipwrecked and ended up on an island. The inhabitants of this island perhaps looked different. It's interesting that Paul says in the book of Romans that he was obligated to Barbarians, people who were different, people who were foreigners.

Do you realize you have foreigners here in Grand Island, Nebraska? Nebraska is a very different looking state than it was 15 years ago when I moved here. God has brought the world to Nebraska. You see people coming in from Bosnia, North Africa, Southeast Asia, Central America, and Mexico. According to the latest census, there are a number of cities in this state, small towns included, that have around a 50-percent Hispanic population.

As I travel the state, I might expect to hear, "Well, great! Hispanics are coming to Nebraska." No way. Instead, I find racial tension, hostility, and anger. God has the right to bring to this state whomever he desires.

We have a problem with Mexicans in Nebraska, don't we? We don't want to admit it, but we do. See, this is confusing. A lot of our churches are involved in programs that send youngsters to Mexico to minister the gospel, build homes, feed the poor, to live out the Great Commission. It's a wonderful thing; let's keep doing it. But what happens when God brings the foreign mission project right here to Nebraska? Why do we have a problem when Mexico comes here? Isn't that why we went to Mexico? Or, is it that we might like the trip more than we like the people. You see, anyone who claims to know God but still has prejudice for people in his/her heart had better question their faith. Because, you know what, like father like son, like father like daughter. This kind of prejudice is not like our heavenly Father.

Paul, who desired to be like his heavenly Father, was obliged not only to the Greeks and Barbarians, people who were very different from himself, but he was also obligated to those who were wise as well as to those who were foolish. The word wise in the Old Testament was a Hebrew word translated *hokma,* which meant skilled in godly living. Foolish would be just the opposite, unskilled in godly living.

When you study the Bible to learn how Jesus treated people, you will find something unusual. He hung out with prostitutes, tax collectors, and sinful people of all sorts, the dregs of the earth. He was gentle, gracious, merciful, and loving to them. When they came and sat at His feet, they found mercy, grace, and forgiveness the same way anybody here who has come to Christ, including myself, has found mercy, grace, and forgiveness. We have to love and open our arms to all people.

God's Rescue Mission For You

God loves people so much that He is on a rescue mission to save each of us from an eternity in Hell. God's love is like this. Let's say I go to the state fair. I have my wife, my six-year-old daughter, Sojourner, and my two-year-old daughter, Bronwyn, with me. Now, Bronwyn is two years old, so we put her in a stroller and wrap her up pretty good. She is not going anywhere. Sojourner, well, you can't hook a six-year-old up like that, so she walks around. We're always saying, "Sojourner, stay close, stay close." We always have to keep our eye on her. At the end of the night we have had a great time. People are still milling around. All of a sudden, we turn our heads and Sojourner has disappeared into the night. My wife looks at me in a panic and says, "Ron, where is Sojourner? Where did she go?" I look at her very calmly with a smile on my face and say, "Honey, don't worry about it. No problem. So what if Sojourner is lost. We still have Bronwyn."

You think that would fly? No way. I'd sit my wife and Bronwyn down and tell them not to move. Then, I would begin to search madly for my little girl. I would ask questions. I would turn over tables. I would be yelling, "Sojourner, where are you? Come back to daddy; please come home." I would tear the fairgrounds to pieces until I found my little girl. You sense my urgency, don't you? Then, when I found her huddled in a corner, scared and shaken and full of shame that she ran away from her daddy, I would pick her up, put her in my arms, love her, kiss her, and hold her and I would laugh and I would cry. We would bounce around. I would put her on my shoulders, and we would go back to where Mommy and Bronwyn were. Then we would celebrate some more. You see, that's the picture God has for you. He's on a rescue mission for you, and He's got people on an all out search for you.

God's love for you is also like this: God has a picture of you on His heavenly refrigerator. He stares at it every day and says, "I love you." For some of you, He is saying, "Where are you? Why have you been running from Me?" Some of you here tonight have been running from God. You are lost and huddled up in shame under some table, afraid of meeting God, thinking that you don't deserve to be found. But, God wants to pick you up and love you with all His might, fill you with His intimacy, and you will be obliged forever. You know what? When you have been found like that, you will be obliged forever.

What is your position?

Because God had found, saved and loved

Paul, he knew he was obliged to serve. Paul knew who he was as a servant. In verse 15, Paul goes on with another *I am,* and here's where it's going to get pretty intense. Paul says this: "So for my part, I am eager to preach the gospel to you also who are in Rome." Not only was Paul eager to serve people, but he was eager to shout the truth. He said, ". . . for my part." Do you realize that you and I have a part? Do you realize there is a place on God's team for you? If a freshmen football player at Nebraska joins our team without a position they might wander around asking, "What meetings do I go to? What position do I line up for?" It is very confusing for a player who doesn't know his position, but I will tell you, and I believe this is true, that most of the people on this earth walk around and really don't know what part they have. They don't know what position God has called them to. Many of us are existing on a survival mode. We show up and hope to get through another day, hope to earn a living, hope to get through another day of school. But, God has so much more for us.

Many of us are searching for our role in

life. Do you realize God passed out talents, gifts, and skills just for you? He didn't just slap you together. It wasn't a big bang theory. It was a delicate procedure when he made you and formed you in the womb of your mother. That is exactly what he did. God has given you something that no one has ever had in the entire world or will ever have. It's a special unique package just for you. It's incredible. Do you realize that people would not take their lives if they understood that? People would not pour foreign substances down their throats if they understood that. People would be excited and eager about life.

Paul said, "I am eager to preach the gospel" because Paul realized his gift was preaching the gospel. That's why he was eager to preach. How many eager people do you see today? Life has just sucked the air right out of them. A lot of us are like that. We're like a piece of paper. We get crunched up in life, and we're feeling all wrinkled up.

You know what God wants to do? He wants to fill you up with His air. He's got a plan and a purpose for you. People like that are eager to get up in the morning. They don't roll around and toss around in bed all day long. They get up. They get after it. They are excited about life. Are you that way? I tell you, some of you here just dread tomorrow, just dread it. You hate your job, and you're really not satisfied with your family. Perhaps you're afraid of what you will meet at school. But Paul says, "I am eager" because he was filled up with God.

As you read through Scripture, Paul tells us that he was hard to hear. For heaven's sake, the guy preached sermons way too long. One kid fell asleep during one of Paul's sermons, fell out the window, and died. So, Paul went down there and prayed him up from the dead, then went back up and preached into the wee hours of the morning. It wasn't always a delightful thing to hear Paul, but do you know what? Every time Paul preached, something was happening. It was either a riot or a revival. After Paul spoke, things happened and that's why he loved it. He recognized he had the truth, so he was eager to preach the gospel to those who were also in Rome.

In Rome, did you hear what I said? In Rome! Do you realize what Rome meant to a Christian? Rome hated Christ and hated any messenger of the good news of Christ. When Paul said, "I am eager to preach the gospel in Rome," what he was saying was, "I am willing to lay my neck on the line. I know it might cost my life, but I am eager to come and bring forth to you the Word of Life." He was eager about that.

Do you realize that we live in a modern-day *Rome?* Do you realize there is a culture out there that hates Christ, hates his followers? Do you realize that if you're a Christian and you love the Lord Jesus Christ, it's costly for you to open your mouth up in the public square? Many of us are silent in *Rome* because we are afraid of what the world thinks. Some of us are supposedly strong Christians, but we don't have the guts to speak it out in public. We speak out in our little churches and our little nooks and crannies in the Christian community, but we also need impact players in *Rome.* We need people who are willing to put on the pads and helmet and go out there in front of the world and speak out.

Let me tell you something. A Christian who wants to keep his faith private is like a football player who joins the huddle but never leaves it. Can you imagine going to a Husker game, the Huskers line up in the huddle, and that's where they stay? Nobody breaks the huddle! What a terrible game that would be.

You know what? There is an ugly opponent waiting for us, too. We get the truth in the huddle, we get fellowship in the huddle, we get energized in the huddle, and we come out and do some serious battle. That's how you live, right? You say you aren't living that way? You aren't willing to go public in *Rome?*

We usually get married in front of people. We graduate in front of people. I guarantee you, many parents here are going to send out announcements that say, "Come to our graduation party and bring presents." Right? We go public. We go public with our football team. We're not on closed circuit TV, we are on national TV. We don't have a closed stadium where we don't invite people in. We encourage people to come. We go public with all these things, many which are really not that important when you think about it. So, are we going to keep silent and be private about the most important thing of all? Who says we have to be private about our faith? Paul was eager to shout out his faith, to shout out the gospel.

Dan Alexander was a guy that I really admired at Nebraska, a great running back for us. Tennessee drafted him today in the NFL. I got the opportunity to recruit Dan. I have known him since he was a junior in high school. Every day that I have known Dan, he has been very eager about his faith, eager to be very intentional about his faith. Now, Dan is not very loud; but he shares his faith and lives it out.

Every day in practice, you could see Dan's faith out on that field. Dan Alexander intentionally lived out his faith. I will give you one example of how he did that. Every day during his career at Nebraska we got a five minute break in the middle of practice to get a little Gatorade and water just to replenish the fluids we had lost. Dan would be the first one over to the water table. Now, if you have never seen Dan Alexander, he is 6-foot-1, 257 pounds, and he has four-percent body fat. This guy is put together. Dan Alexander runs the 40-yard dash in 4.4

seconds. Now that is flying! That is faster than most track runners in your high school. He can fly! That big body can roll, and you know what? He rolls it when it's break time. He is the first one over to the water table. Who is going to outrun Dan? If someone does try to beat Dan to the table, who is going to elbow Dan for that water?

But do you know what really happens? When Dan gets there, his helmet comes off, he smiles, and he starts handing out cups of Gatorade and water to every one of our players and coaches. Then, on hot days, he hands out seconds and thirds for those guys. There have been days when I think Dan hasn't gotten any water or Gatorade to drink for himself. Every day he does the same thing. What's he doing? I talked to Dan about this. I said, "Dan, what's up with that?" I already knew but I wanted to hear him say it. He said, "Coach, it is a witness, a witness of my faith."

Dan knows that one day these men are not going to have 76,000 people clapping for them anymore, and he knows that one day some of them are going to be sitting in a marriage that is falling apart, and many of them will be looking for pain relievers in life, feeling hopeless and anguished. Dan recognizes that there are lost guys on our football team who need the Gospel. Without saying one word about Jesus while he is handing out these cups, he is passing them a cup of cool refreshment in Christ, and those players know it. They know why. They know of Dan's love for Jesus. Dan is intentional, and one day when a player is sitting at the brink of an abyss in his life and is ready to do something crazy, ready to throw away his marriage or throw away his life, he might remember that big smiling muscular guy on the football team named Dan Alexander, a born-again Christian who loved the Lord with all his heart. He might remember Dan Alexander passing out a cool refreshment in Jesus, being intentional about his faith. It may very well connect him with the hope that we have in Christ.

Do you realize every one of us here has an opportunity to share our faith in Christ by the little things we do: encouraging letters, a pat on the back to somebody, forgiveness after a long period of tension? If you are on a rescue mission, you will do anything to save the lost. You realize where they are going to end up.

Don't Flinch on Alcohol!

However, there are times in *Rome* when we have to open up our mouths and speak up as well. I know because *Rome* has told me personally to shut up in the public square. Let me give you some examples. They say, "Coach Brown, come out to our little town in Nebraska. Help us say no to drugs." I show up. I start talking about the most prevalent drug I know, the most addictive substance I know, alcohol. "Wait a minute, Brown, we didn't mean alcohol. We meant the real stuff." That real stuff is bad, too, but alcohol is *Rome's* favorite beverage. People are always trying to shove alcohol down my throat. I've decided personally not to drink alcohol. Ask these questions: What good is it really doing? Are these people who are always trying to stick alcohol down my throat concerned about my thirst? Well, you know, H_2O will do it every time. Water is safe. Are they concerned about my taste buds? No, a milk shake or lemonade will do. They are safe. I can get behind the wheel of a car, and I won't do any harm to anybody. Why is it that *Rome* wants to stick alcohol down my throat all the time? I believe it's a pain reliever. That's right. Here in America we love pain relievers, don't we? Get a little headache, take a pain reliever.

Some of you may feel like you are getting your toes stepped on. You know what? I didn't come here to tiptoe through the tulips. I will tell you straight up. If you are thinking alcohol is an okay substance, let me give you some stats here to show you how "okay" it is. Alcohol costs Americans 136 billion dollars per year. More than 65,000 lives are lost per year due to alcohol, 22,000 of them on the highways. Twenty percent of all deaths by freezing are due to alcohol. Twenty-five percent of choking deaths, eighty percent of falling deaths, fifty-two percent of fire related deaths, sixty percent of suicides, sixty-four percent of murders, sixty-nine percent of drownings, seventy-six percent of aircraft deaths, seventy-two percent of robbery and assaults, sixty percent of rapes, and eighty percent of criminal court cases in this country are related to alcohol.

Maybe you think, "Well, we are here in Nebraska. We don't have it like that." I had somebody check the Nebraska Drug and Alcohol Counsel for me. We were able to get statistics for Nebraska. Do you realize that just a couple years ago 56 percent of Nebraska high school students consumed alcohol compared to 52 percent nationally? We're above the national average. Do you know that 47 percent of Nebraska twelfth graders admitted to driving after they had been drinking alcohol? According to this poll, almost half of the kids here in the state of Nebraska have admitted to getting in a car and driving after they had been drinking alcohol!

Some of you parents may not know that Nebraska is number two in the nation behind Montana in youth binge drinking. Do you realize what binge drinking is? It's taking several drinks in a row, just guzzling them down, drinking to get blasted, to get drunk. They call Nebraska "the good life." This is the good life? If it's such a good life, why do our teenagers pour *Rome's* favorite drink down their throats at a rate above the national average?

Something is missing inside, and I have to admit I am part of the problem. Turn on a nationally televised Nebraska football game and you'll see numerous advertisements promoting alcohol. I feel bad about that. It's a shame that children and you have to endure the content of these commercials. These commercials often show good-looking people, some with their shirts off and their muscles rippling. I guess if you drink a lot of beer, you get a body like that. Yeah, that's what *Rome* would like you to think, but do they ever broadcast commercials showing students on prom night, drinking, then getting into a car? Suddenly, the car veers off into a telephone pole, smashes up and the students are killed. The bodies are so badly smeared to the steering wheel and windshield that it takes hours for the authorities to get them out. Do they ever show you that commercial? No, *Rome* won't show you that one.

How about this one? A man has had a long day at work. Matter of fact, it has been a long year at work. Things aren't going well on the job. He is wondering who he really is. His wife and children are at home, but he just doesn't feel like coming home tonight. So, he stops off at the local tavern after work with his buddies. No harm in that, right, guys? It's okay to knock a few down. Finally, he checks his watch and realizes he'd better go home. As he pulls up in the driveway, his wife and children are waiting for him. They want to know where he's been. It's way after the time he is normally home. He just doesn't feel like dealing with it. Then in a fit of rage, he takes it out physically on his wife and his children. We don't see this all-too-familiar scene because it is carried on behind closed doors, window drapes and shades, but it happens over and over and over again in this country, in this state, in this city.

Some of you come from homes like that. You have learned to put on some phony-bologna smile when you walk out of those doors, as if all is well when you know it is a living hell inside.

If you still aren't convinced, put yourself in this scene. Let's say you are having brain surgery tomorrow. Your doctor asks you this question: "Your operation is a very delicate, intense one. To calm me down, would you mind if I drank a few martinis before we begin? How about a few beers? Would that be okay?" I don't think you would go for that.

Don't Flinch on Sexual Immorality!

Rome says to me, "Shut up about sex, Brown. Don't talk about waiting until you're married to have sex. These kids don't understand that. That is very unrealistic." Three years ago a study was made of prime time TV shows between the hours of 7 pm to 10 pm. The study reported that approximately 2000 television episodes illustrated sexual behavior during these prime time hours. Of these 2000 shows illustrating sexual behavior, eighty percent of them depicted people who were unmarried.

Basically, *Rome* says it is okay to be unmarried and have sex. Let's pick on coaches for a minute and talk about the show "Coach." This was a popular TV show. Isn't it interesting that the coach was living with a woman? I guess they got married in a later episode, but for a long time he was living with a woman and, of course, they were enjoying a sexual relationship.

America seems to glue itself to that type of show. TV is like a vacuum cleaner; it sucks us right up into it. Then we buy into its messages. It normalizes something that God says is abnormal. He says to wait to have sex until you're married. The Bible is God's playbook. It contains the truth, the whole truth, and nothing but the truth, so help us God. Yes, the playbook of life says, "Don't run that play until you are married." It's a wonderful play when you are married. Sex is a beautiful thing. I have two beautiful daughters who were created through a loving act of sexual intimacy with my wife. That's one of the reasons God gave us that gift, for procreation of children, but He also gave it to us for marital pleasure. Sex is designed for marriage between a man and a woman. You see, it is something that only those two are supposed to enjoy together, and you know what, God also created sex to feel good. Some of you are blushing. Sex is suppose to feel good because it is a symbol for the third reason God created sex. He wants us to enjoy sex because it is the symbolic union of Christ marrying his church. It shows that precious, loving, intimate relationship between Christ and his church. So, every time we engage in the act of sexual intimacy with our husband or wife, it should remind us of God.

If that's the truth, then why does *Rome* spend astronomical amounts of money per year on pornography? Why are Americans buying it? Many Christians are addicted to pornography, including pastors. Many pastors have been dethroned from their platforms of ministry because of pornography. I have talked to a number of inmates who are in jail on rape charges, and a pornographic magazine triggered their problem.

Some of you young ladies here tonight want to remain virgins until you are married. That is a wonderful thing that God has ordained for you. Virginity is a special gift you present before God at the altar. You present your body, your virginity, to God who expects virginity for a man as well as a woman. I am ashamed that men in my generation have done a horrible job of teaching our sons that virginity is the most masculine thing they can do before they are married. We talk to our boys about fishing and hunting, football, and fixing cars and we say that is masculine. The most masculine think we can teach our boys is control, control of their bodies because they recognize that God is on the throne.

Young ladies, do you want a young man who is trying to sweet talk you into giving up that portion of your life before you are married? *Rome* tells you "go for it." Your girlfriends tell you, "Go for it: we've tried it." That special dreamboat guy says, "If you really love me, you will go for it." Well, that guy is a coward. He is a weakling. Do you want that kind of man? Or, do you want a man who is strong? You want a man who knows who is on the throne. That is the guy you can trust. Who is to say if he cannot control himself with you, that he is going to control himself with someone else when the whim comes along.

Young ladies, let me say this to you. Too many rapes are taking place in this country. I understand that type of sex is forced upon you against your will, but in most other cases of sexual intimacy you have the final say. Do you understand that the sexual diseases and pregnancies that come before marriage, in most cases, come from the consent of a woman? You need to be strong. You first "marry" Jesus, and then He will pick that right guy for you at the right time.

Young men, let me tell you now, you stand strong for Christ. There will be rewards at the end of it. If you buy into the lie of *Rome,* those lies will self-destruct you. I guarantee it.

Health professionals say, "Well, look, kids shouldn't hear that Brown bologna about chastity and abstinence. What an unrealistic, intolerant message. These kids can't handle that. They need Plan B. They are going to have sex no matter what you say to them." I say, "Wait a minute. Are these kids dogs, cows, sheep and pigs? No, they are not creatures of instinct. God gave them a soul, the ability to say 'yes' to the things that are right and 'no' to the things that are wrong. We raise the standard high, and these young people can meet it." The problem is most of us in *Rome* are silent. We won't tell them the truth.

Now, if these health professionals were really honest with you, they would have to tell you there is a 16 to 20 percent failure rate in all the devices they hand out as Plan B for safe sex. There is no such thing as safe sex for unwanted pregnancy or sexual disease. Most of you drive cars. If you had a 16 to 20 percent failure rate in your car engine, would you turn on the ignition knowing it might blow up on you? I tell you this: we pass those odds out to our kids and say, "Let's go for it." Hog wash!

The reason I am so passionate about this topic is because I am a product of sexual indiscretion. I have never known my birth parents. My birth parents decided to engage in that kind of an act. I was that conception, and I ended up in an orphanage in New York City with a bunch of other inner city kids in the same situation, kids that nobody wanted, who didn't know who they were. By the grace of God, I stand here before you today. Somebody came along and called me *son*. Two people old enough to be my grandparents gave me a chance. I'm angry— angry that there are kids all over this country who don't know who their birth parents are because people have decided to do their own thing and run their own plays. That's a reason why we have so many malfunctions in the body of Christ today. Even Christians have multiple partners. We buy into *Rome's* deceitful lie. Jesus was born and grew up on this earth. The Bible says when he was a teenager; he lived for God and grew in wisdom and stature. That same Jesus who lives in your child can help him/her to do the same thing. That's the standard we need to raise for our kids.

Don't Flinch on Homosexuality!

Rome also tells me to shut up about homosexuality. I got in big trouble for talking about homosexuality a couple of years ago. I spoke on my Christian radio show rebuking fellow Christians and myself for the way we have treated homosexuals—when we discard them, not wanting anything to do with them. We don't invite them to church with us. We don't invite them to Bible study. We don't pray for them. We just disdain them.

That is not the loving attitude of Christ. Christ loves every one of them. He loves every one of us. Every one of us came through the same door of grace. No one is a greater sinner than the other is, but it is true that homosexuality is a sin. On my radio show, I said that we don't endorse the sin, but we love the sinner.

When *Rome* heard me say that homosexuality is a sin, they tried to hang me. They came at me with big hammers trying to silence me. You know, it is interesting. They came into the Christian context to get me. I wasn't out there on a platform on top of the roof with a blow horn blaring that homosexuality is a sin, saying "Come media, come hear me." No, I was speaking on a five minute Christian radio program, bought and paid for by Christian people who love the message of Christ. *Rome* heard it, pulled it out of the Christian context, and stuck it up in the public market place to be smeared. That's how the world of *Rome* operates.

Do you understand that there are no more hiding places for the Christian? *Rome* will come and get you, but we shouldn't be running and hiding, anyway. We should be out there in *Rome* eager to preach the gospel. Homosexuality is a sin. Says who? Says God. God tells us in the Old Testament in Leviticus 18 that homosexuality is a sin.

Then, in the New Testament in Romans 1, 1 Timothy 1, and 1 Corinthians 6, God clearly states again that homosexuality is a sin. There is no doubt about it, but *Rome* doesn't want to hear that.

Don't Flinch on Abortion!

Rome says to shut up about abortion; in fact, the "powers to be" suggest that there are two things you don't talk about. You don't talk about homosexuality and you don't talk about abortion. Well, I just finished talking about homosexuality, and now I am getting ready to talk about abortion. Abortion is murder. I realize it is costly to say that. Take all I have, take anything you want, but count me in on the fight against abortion.

When I looked into the sonograms taken of both my girls before their births, I saw little fingers moving around. I saw a little button nose. I saw a heart beating on that monitor. Today, those little girls assault their daddy when I come home. They knock me down and kiss me and love me. Man, that's life. You know guys; you have felt your wife's tummy when she was pregnant. You felt a little kicking and you said, "That's my little linebacker getting ready to come out." Then you went to the hospital, the baby popped out, the doctor caught it and the baby cried. Man, what a sound! What a beautiful sound as a child enters into this world, but do you realize that tomorrow as you go to work or school there will be 10 such babies removed from the wombs of mothers here in the state of Nebraska and executed. Their little heads, squashed like grapes; some burned alive. On the average, ten babies per day are aborted in the state of Nebraska. Instead of murder, *Rome* calls it a medical procedure or a woman's choice. What a horrible thing: four to five thousand babies are aborted here in the state of Nebraska per year.

Now I tell you, the Holocaust in Nazi Germany was a horrific thing, a terrible thing. Adolph Hitler murdered over 6 million Jews simply because they were Jewish. Joseph Stalin murdered over 10 million people in a political cleansing. But, the greatest numerical holocaust in the history of the world began in 1973 with the Roe vs Wade decision right here in the land of the free and the home of the brave, in

America. Read through Scripture, which has to be the source of our truth. In the books of Isaiah and Jeremiah, God repeats, "I formed you in the womb." Does Luke 2:5 say "Mary was great with tissue?" No. Does it say, "Mary was great with fetus?" No. It says, "Mary was great with child." That's right. God says there was a child in Mary's womb.

What if we took one-day-old babies and gunned them down with a machine gun? There would be a whole lot of talking in *Rome,* wouldn't there? In the meantime, babies are being executed daily on the other side of the birth canal. Can you hear their cries in *Rome?* Do you hear them screaming and kicking as you are going to work or school? Those screaming, kicking babies fighting for their lives should break your heart because they break God's heart. What breaks God's heart even more is the silence of Christians who live in *Rome* and won't speak up.

Don't Flinch on Witnessing!

Rome says shut up in the public school about your faith. They say, "When you come to buildings like this, don't talk about your faith in Christ. That's a no-no. That's off limits. You keep it secular here. Do what you want with your Christian thing in your church." Well, you know what? When the blood of Jesus poured off of him, I was at the foot of the cross and the blood fell all over me. Because His blood covers me, I can't separate myself from Christ.

When I walk into a public school, I have to admit I feel nervous. I feel the pressure. There is a little voice that says, "Brown, you can't talk about your faith in Christ. They asked you to talk about character. I mean, come on now, don't conjure up something just to share your faith. Do what they asked you to do. If you don't agree with what they ask you to do, then don't accept the speaking engagement." Then another voice says, "Wait a minute, Ron. They asked you to speak about character. Where does character come from? Aren't you supposed to reference the source in public schools? If a student were to do a written report on a particular subject and used someone else's material, wouldn't he/she have to reference the source before handing in the report? If he/she doesn't, the student would get in big trouble. It's called plagiarism.

Because the answers to forming character are not my own, I must credit the source. Let me explain. I am noticing a trend in America. Kids are lying; they are stealing, and they are cheating. When I noticed these trends, I didn't say, "You know what? I think I am going to come up with some rules. Let's say ten of them. I think I'll call them commandments." Do you think the Ten Commandments came from me or someone else on earth? They came from God. God Almighty. That's why the Christian who is asked to speak on character in a public school or any place in the public square not only has the right to speak about his or her faith in Christ, but also has the responsibility to do so. Don't you understand, you can't take credit for the answers to strong moral character? You must reference the Source, and that is exactly what I do.

Let's say I was to take you to the Empire State Building in New York City. For those of you who haven't seen the Empire State Building, it is taller than any silo you see here in Nebraska. It's tall, real tall. What if I took you to the top floor, opened the window, and said, "Jump!" How many of you would do that? I don't think you would do that because you understand there is a law out there called gravity. Isaac Newton didn't create it; he discovered what God had created. Because of gravity, jumping from the top of the Empire State Building would take you to your sure death.

However, what if someone said, "Wait a minute Brown, that's your version of the truth. We have our own version of the truth. Who says there is only one truth? How can you be so intolerant? We think that you can get on top of the Empire State Building, and if you hold your hands and feet in the right position with the right technique, you can actually float to the ground."

How many of you would believe that? But, what if people started to buy into that nonsense? What if people began to say, "Hey, who says there is only one truth? Maybe there is another truth. This theory sounds like it's possible." What if the media started to buy into it? What if TV sitcoms portrayed actors jumping from tall buildings, holding their hands and feet out straight and believably floating safely to the ground? Suppose that some kids started to believe this new idea?

What if I went into the public schools and said, "Wait a minute, don't believe that stuff you see on TV or that you are reading about. It's wrong. You will fall from the top floor of the Empire State Building if you leap out." All of a sudden, the ACLU shows up and starts to write me up and says, "This guy, Brown, is intolerant and bigoted. He is confusing these kids. Who says there is only one truth?" What if my job was on the line for it? What if everybody started to buy into the nonsense that you could float out of the top floor of the Empire State Building? Would that change the truth? I'll tell you what would happen if people dared to jump off the top floor of the Empire State Building to see if they could float. I don't care what they did with their hands and feet; they would fall to their deaths. Why? Because the truth always prevails; that's why.

Do you understand what we are talking about today? The reason why we are eager, or should be eager, to preach the gospel in *Rome* is because God's truth will prevail.

That's why we are on the winning team. That's why I go into a public school even though the administrators and the teachers are all nervous because big mouth Brown might say that horrible word *Jesus.* You know what? I don't disappoint them. Do you know why? Because I see a bunch of kids standing on the top ledge of truth ready to leap into eternity thinking somehow, some way, by their own definition they will just float their way into God's arms, when really they are going to fall to their spiritual death, apart from Christ forever. Therefore, I am going to do everything I can to get them down from the ledge, and that should be the rescue mission for every one of us.

Don't Flinch on Suffering!

We move on to verse 16. Paul was so understanding, so impassioned, so convinced of his purpose, that he was willing to suffer for that message. He says this in Romans 1:16, "For I am not ashamed of the gospel, for it is the power of God for salvation to everyone who believes."

Now, Paul was saying this: "You know

what? Not only will I serve Jesus Christ; not only will I shout out the truth in Rome, but I am also willing to suffer. I am not going to flinch. I'm going to run right through that tackle.

The story of Cassie Bernall, one of the victims of the Columbine High School shooting tragedy, is a powerful example of a person who was so impassioned, so convinced of who she was in Christ that she was willing to suffer for her faith! On April 20, 1999, two teenage boys who had been cleverly deceived by *Rome* entered Columbine High School in Littleton, Colorado, a suburb of Denver, with guns and explosives and gunned down fellow students and teachers. It was a nightmarish thing that could happen anywhere—even right here in Grand Island, Nebraska.

About two weeks after the shooting, I was recruiting in Denver. I was on an airplane coming back from Denver and sitting next to one of Cassie Bernall's best friends. She saw me reading the Bible, and she began to talk about things of the Lord and about her relationship with Cassie. At the age of 15, Cassie was involved heavily with the occult and witchcraft. Her parents were Christians, and recognizing her problems, grounded her. During the time she was grounded, Cassie realized she was lost and needed a Savior. She trusted her life to Jesus Christ and received eternal life. From that point on, her lifestyle changed. She became very intimate with God. She began to read her Bible. Two years later on April 18, Cassie stood up in front of her church congregation and read a poem she had written to God. Two days later on April 20, Cassie, not knowing what was about to take place, walked into that school building. She had her Bible with her. She took a Bible in the public school. She sat down in the library and was reading her Bible when the killers burst in.

We now know that the killers had it in for certain groups of people. One of the categories they were looking for was athletes. Aren't athletes the mighty heroes of our culture? We stick microphones in their faces to hear their words of wisdom. Aren't they the heroes and protectors? Where were these mighty heroes that day when these killers came in? They were running and hiding under tables; that's where they were. Why? Because athletics is not worth dying for, that's why.

But, they were also looking for another category of people. They were looking for people who pursue God. They were looking for Christians. Cassie's friend told me that she thought that Cassie knew these two killers because of the lifestyle she had lived before. Her friend thought Cassie had hung out with them and that they also knew of her conversion. When they came in, they asked if there was anyone in there who believed in God. People were running for their lives, diving under tables, screaming, yelling, and panicking. But there she was, 17 years old, a two-year-old babe in Christ. She stood up and said, "Yes, I believe in God." Bang! They shot and killed her on the spot. Now you tell me, what would possess a 17-year-old girl to stand up and take a bullet? Why didn't she negotiate for her life? She could have begged for mercy. She could have renounced God even for a moment and then taken Him back. What would cause Cassie to stand and die? I tell you what I believe. Cassie had died long before she walked into that school that day. She had died to *Rome*. She had died to her possessions. She had died to the applause of men and women. She died to the false shame that comes from living publicly for Christ. She died for all the right reasons. When she walked in that day, there was a young woman who lived intimately with Christ, who was intentional about her faith. She stood up and in a sense said, "Count me in. I say 'no' to *Rome,* and I say 'yes' to Jesus!"

Every time I hear that story I am ashamed because I have been a silent Christian too many times in *Rome,* afraid of losing my reputation, let alone my life. Here is a young woman, a two-year-old babe in Christ, willing to stand up. Today she lives forever and ever next to God, the one she died for. This is a beautiful thing.

I came here tonight to ask you this question. Are you prepared to die? Just as there is a Heaven, there is also a Hell. Do you know that Jesus talked more about Hell than he talked about Heaven? What if you had a Scrooge-like experience tonight, and God could take you to Heaven, open the window, and have you just peek in? You would see Cassie. You would see people who gave their lives to Christ partying, high-fiving one another, praising God forever and ever and ever. What an incredible sight. You would say, "This is it. I want to go to Heaven." God would look at you and say, "No, we are not done yet. We still have some living to do." Then He would take you to that *other* place. Now some of you may be very skeptical about Hell because some way, somehow, *Rome* wants you to believe there is no such thing as Hell. *Rome* wants you to believe that you can jump out of any window you want and you will float into the arms of God. Well, *Rome* wants you to believe a lie. Yes, there is a Heaven, but there is also a Hell.

When Jesus talked about Hell, he was very descriptive. In Luke 16, Jesus talked about a man who was burning in an eternal fire. Do you realize that once you die, you will never again be in a state of unconsciousness? You'll always experience either excruciating pain or incredible joy forever and ever and ever and ever. It will never end. Going to Hell is like being tortured forever but never dying. You know those spy movies where they are torturing the spy and you say, "Man, I wish they would just kill him and put him out of his misery," but instead they just keep torturing him. That's how it is in Hell. I've heard some people say, "I will take my chances. I will be down there with my friends." Hell is a lonely place. The Bible says it is a place of outer darkness. It is a place of weeping and wailing. I'm not talking about boo-hoo the Huskers got beat or boo-hoo my boyfriend broke up with me. I'm talking about screaming, wailing and weeping, and gnashing of the teeth. Jesus said people will feel regrets inside, such as "Why didn't I listen when I was on earth? I had the opportunity. I heard the gospel, and I rejected it. How could I have done that?" But, once you are in Hell, it's too late.

You say, "God, I don't want to go to Hell." God will answer by taking you to a scene that took place some 700-800 years before Christ was born. Isaiah, through the inspiration of God's Holy Spirit, is predicting the death of Jesus. Isaiah wrote this prediction in Isaiah 52:14. Isaiah said that Jesus would be beaten like no man had ever been beaten. Seven hundred to eight hundred years later, that came true. The New Testament says that Jesus was unrecognizable as he hung on the cross. First, He was dealt heavy blows to the face, buffeted over and over again. The Roman crucifixion process was horrible. After Jesus was beaten, he was lashed many times with a whip that consisted of several leather strips that had pieces of jagged glass and metal, with sheep skin knuckles tied to the ends. Those skillful Roman guards would snap their wrists down and then back again, ripping back with it flesh, tissue, and muscle off the bone. Historians say between the eighteenth and the twenty-fifth lash you could begin to see a man's bones. But this was not some hardened criminal. This is the innocent Lord. Psalm 22 says that Jesus' bones were exposed. What a bloody mess lying there!

Some of our football players at Nebraska think they are a bunch of strong guys. They can handle anything. Some of them think Christianity is for wimps and it will make them soft. They don't want anything to do with Christ while they are playing. That's for later, when they are old. They don't understand that two-thirds of the people who were whipped like that died right there. They didn't get up. Only one-third got up. Jesus got up. He was tough physically, mentally, emotionally, and spiritually. He was going to the cross and nothing was going to stop him. He was thinking about every single one of us. Blood was pouring down his back as he hoisted a 175-pound cross upon his back and carried it up the hill where he was to be crucified. Finally, He spread out his arms and allowed the Romans to drive massive nails through His wrists into the wooden beam. Then His ankles were crossed, and a nail was once again driven through flesh and bone into the wooden cross.

Now, He was God. He could have gotten out of this at anytime. He chose, instead, to live as a man, the God-man, to suffer as a man in our place. He was probably dehydrated and in metabolic shock, heaving, vomiting, suffering pain and agony. He hung on that cross for six hours. Our big, strong, football players complain about five minutes of wind sprints after practice. But, as Christ looked down, where were all of his followers? Many of them left Him. You know what? When you devote your life to Christ, many are going to leave you. That's right. You are going to spend some lonely moments, but I will tell you this. God the Father never left Him, and He will never leave you. As He hung on, He thought about every single one of us. That's what breaks my heart. It breaks my heart to know that someone loved me that much. Some of you have never experienced that kind of love before, and you are searching for love in all the wrong places. The square pegs of *Roman* culture do not fit the round holes of emptiness, and you are looking for pain relievers. Christ is the answer, the greatest relief of all, and the only solution. He died on a cross in the flesh to pay a price for the penalty of sin that had to be paid for us to have a relationship with Him and eternal life.

You have a choice to make before you walk out of here tonight. You are going to make one of two choices. Either you are going to reject Christ, or you are going to follow Him. If you reject Him, you are Hell bound. There is no guarantee you are going to get a chance to hear the gospel again. There is no guarantee that you will even live through the night. I have spoken with numerous audiences over the last fifteen years in Nebraska. It is amazing the number of times that people have written me after an event saying, "Coach Brown, would you send a card to the family of a seventeen-year-old boy who had been to an event like this and later died in a car crash? or telling me to pray for the family of a forty-year-old school teacher who recently heard a message like this and shortly thereafter, died of a massive heart attack." None of us here are promised tomorrow. In an audience this large, statistically speaking, there is a good chance somebody in the near future is going to die, and you don't know who it is. God has your days numbered. You cannot dictate your life; you cannot control your life.

If you decide to live for *Rome,* you might as well go for it 100 percent. Choosing to reject Jesus is like walking on the white stripe in the middle of the highway to see how close cars and trucks are going to get to you before somebody hits you and kills you. You will get hit and die apart from Christ. I want to tell you something tonight. Hearts can become hardened to Christ's offer of salvation. You hear the message and you don't respond. Your heart doesn't come back softer; it comes back harder.

Tonight, if you know there is something going on inside, if you know you are not prepared to die, if you know that if you died tonight you would not go to Heaven, you are playing with danger by walking out of this building. I will tell you another thing. Don't leave this building tonight questioning whether you are saved or not. What if someone said to me "Coach Brown, are you married?" And I said, "I don't know." Well, the reason I do know I'm married is that on July 29, 1984, we made it public. I covenanted with Molvina before God Almighty that this is my wife. This is my mate for life, so help us God. We exchanged wedding rings. If someone asked me today, "Are you married?" "Yes, I am married." If you get married to Jesus, you will know. If you don't know, then it never happened. Tonight you can be absolutely sure.

Now, I am going to ask you to strongly consider this: If you are willing to follow Jesus, then I am going to ask you to leave *Rome* behind. I am going to ask you to do exactly what Cassie Bernall did. I am going to ask you, if you have never made that decision before, to get up out of that seat and say, "Yes, count me in." I am going to ask you to come forward in front of *Rome* and say, "Yes, I am willing to follow Jesus." It is your decision. No one is going to make you do it. It is not about me. I am just a messenger. It is about God and you. It's not about your friend. It's not about what your family thinks of you. It's not about trying to get a few points with God tonight.

God wants you to die to *Rome*. He wants you to release *Rome*. Some of you are begging and starving for love, and here it is: Jesus Christ, God in the flesh, came to this earth, died in your place and my place on a cross. They buried Him. He rose from the dead. He conquered death. He gives you new life.

The only way that you can be forgiven for your sins is through a relationship with Christ. Jesus said, "I am the way, the truth and the life. No man comes to the Father but by me." If that's not good enough for you, there is nothing more that can be said tonight.

You take your own chances. I guarantee one day in eternity you will remember this night. You will be on one side of eternity or the other, but you will remember this night. While you have breath in your body tonight, don't turn down this opportunity. God has been on a rescue mission and he has finally found you. Some of you have been running, but you have let yourself be found.

I am going to come down here right now. I am going to fall down on the floor. I am going to be the first fool in this place. This is something that *Rome* tells me is a stupid thing to do. I am going public with it because God went public for me. If you're not willing to go public for God in this building where it is nice and safe, what makes you think you are going to do it out there in *Rome?* You will turn Him down in a minute. I am asking you for the first time in many of your lives to remove the chains from that chair, come up, and meet the Lord Jesus Christ right at the foot of the cross tonight, and Christ will save you. He will give you a new home in Heaven.

I'm going to read a Scripture to let you know for sure that you have a relationship with Jesus Christ, so I ask those of you who have driven to just wait and let people make their decision. There will be serious wrestling matches, one on one battles, going on between Satan and those in this room. Those who know Christ need to be involved in serious spiritual warfare right now in prayer because Satan will do everything he can to cause people in this arena to turn down this opportunity. Some of you know you need a Savior. I ask you to come without hypocrisy before God. He knows the phony bologna. Don't come up here playing games. If you're broken hearted, and you realize you need a Savior, I am asking you to come forward and be a fool for Christ.

I had heard all my life about Jesus Christ. I believed intellectually and conceptually in Him, but I had no relationship with Him. I was living my life on my own, calling my shots, making my own plans, pulling myself up the ladder of success by my own boot-straps until I came to an end of myself one day.

All of these things that I was chasing began to leave me high and dry with an emptiness inside. Some call it a weakness, a crutch. I thank God that I finally realized I was too weak to control life and make it revolve around Ron Brown. Every person, including myself, was too weak to totally fulfill me. I thank God for the 'crutch' that He offered to me as a free gift—the cross of Jesus Christ.

Jesus as God in the flesh came down to earth, lived a sinless life, changed hearts, healed the sick, performed miracles, was crucified on a cross for my sins, then was buried and rose from the grave. That day in 1979, I finally realized only Jesus could give me the love, purpose, and direction on earth as well as the home in Heaven that I wanted so badly. It was then that I banked my life by faith that Jesus rose out of the grave, went back to Heaven and is coming back one day to rule forever. That day I asked Jesus Christ into my heart, I decided to repent and turn from sinful life. Jesus will enter and rule the life of anyone who believes and trusts in Him as Savior and Lord for forgiveness of their sins. That day was the greatest day of my life. It was the day I truly became a winner by joining God's team. Are you prepared for the greatest opportunity of your life?

Please read the following Bible verses that Ron shared with the audience:

John 3:16
Romans 3:23
Romans 6:23
Romans 10:9-13

For more information about spiritual matters, please contact:

Mission Nebraska
PO Box 6225
Lincoln, NE 68506
Phone: 402-489-5018
Fax: 402-441-0631
Email: contact@MissionNebraska.org